DOLL'

"A CHRISTMAS CAROL IN RHYME

by

Christine Burrows

(Story by Charles Dickens, "A Christmas Carol"
Adapted into poetic rhyme)

All characters and events in this publication,
other than those clearly in the public domain,
are fictitious and any resemblance to real persons,
living or dead, is purely coincidental.

Copyright © 2015 Christine Burrows

All rights reserved.

ISBN: 9781517253547

Uncle Scrooge

Now Ebenezer had a dream one night,
four fearful apparitions came to call.
The first one, Jacob Marley gave a fright
when dragging chains and ledgers 'cross the hall.

The second, Christmas past, began to haunt
the fun of yesterday, now dead and gone,
at one a.m. another ghost was caught,
no charity for Scrooge, his meanness won.

The ghost appearing last had chilling news
an early death became his fateful path,
and no one cared about this misers muse,
as at his death, so many people laughed.

The error of his ways was changed in time,
as Scrooge became a man we now think kind.

DEDICATION

For Ken

and

For my daughters who always support me in my
endeavours, no matter how crazy they may seem.

ACKNOWLEDGEMENTS

To
Charles Dickens
who I greatly admire,
and for me, was the greatest
author in Victorian times. He
inspired me with his wit and humour,
powerful literary words and tenacity to write
about how life really was for ordinary people. Also for
his great personal resolve when faced with crisis, and his
innate understanding of human nature. He was a literary genius.
Thanks to him, I was able to adapt his book into rhyming words.

Illustrations by Prawny Vintage

CONTENTS

THE FIRST GHOST
JACOB MARLEY

"He is quite dead! Dead as a dormant nail. . ."
His grasping partner starts our terror tale.
For Scrooge and Marley bitter life extends;
their miserable deeds would have no end.

When Marley died, Scrooge on a mournful course,
continued on with life with no remorse;
a selfish man, now spent his time alone,
his heavy heart was made of solid stone.

Scrooge stooped with age, and stiffened was his gait,
a lonely man, his heart was filled with hate,
with shrivelled cheeks and pointed crooked nose,
a hard demeanour purposely proposed.

It had been seven years, they quickly passed,
the snowy streets were white and icing fast;
a coach and six came galloping-on through,
the carol singers sang, and sleighs just flew.

His counting house was dark and bitter cold,
his clerk was meek, and Scrooge held tight control.
The room was dank, no real good will invested,
this miser was a man greatly detested.

At Christmas time when Scrooge was always grim,
his frosty word, dismissive, full of sin.
his Nephew called and heard old Scrooge convey.
"Bah Humbug" I won't cheer for you this day."

All charity was left without a penny,
he thought 'work houses' places for the many.
His puny purse stayed firm, and tightly shut,
inside his heart was dusty blackened soot.

One freezing night he came to his front door,
his door knob had a face not seen before!
The face was his old partner looking grim,
but he dismissed the vision, rubbed his chin.

He put his nightcap on, sat in his chair,
the candle dim, his chamber was quite bare;
he heard a clanging, like the links of chain,
and bells were ringing out in heightened pain.

The noise so loud, Scrooge wailed, he was in fear,
he shrieked and saw a figure then appear!
The ghost of Jacob Marley, was now here,
and dragging padlocks, ledgers at the rear.

He said three spirits on each night would come,
the first was due when all the bells tolled one;
the second ghost will call tomorrow night,
the third and last would come at twelve midnight.

Old Scrooge thought this was all a silly dream,
believing none of what he had just seen.
The haunting ghosts had made their sad prediction,
and Scrooge was granted no peace or remission.

The Second Ghost
Christmas Past

The curtains parted to the miser's bed,
and face to face was something very dead:
a child-like figure white, and quite disdainful
was floating like a phantom fairy angel.

"I am the Ghost of Christmas that has passed,
now rise and walk with me along this path."
So terrified, old Scrooge with speed, obeyed,
the clock turned back, and he was so afraid.

At school, Scrooge was a very lonely boy,
dejected mostly, and was rather coy,
As all his fervent memories return,
another life when love was his concern.

The festive fun at Fezziwig's great ball,
as "Merry Christmas" shouts to one and all.
The season's gaiety, was full of fun,
the poor were joyous, so was everyone.

Remembering he broke off his engagement
pursuing wealth and fortune, his arrangement,
and Scrooge could hardly bear what he'd become,
his former happy self was clearly gone.

He said: "Why torture me with scenes of joy?
Stop haunting me, my soul you now destroy!
Remove me from this awful tempting place!
I cannot bear this saddened past disgrace."

The spirit said, "These are the truest facts!
This is your past! As history's exact!
Do not blame me for your own stupid folly."
And in his hand, he waved a sprig of holly.

But Scrooge became grief-filled and very tired,
the spirit now was gone, it had expired,
now back to bed, became so very sleepy,
and into slumber, fell so very deeply.

The Third Ghost
Christmas Present

The night was still and as the bell struck one,
his nerves on edge, he knew the ghost would come,
and furtively he paced around the room,
he checked the lock, the ghost would be here soon.

Just then he heard the spirit number two,
he bade him enter, Scrooge just walked on through.
A big surprise then met his wide red eyes,
his room transformed, and was not recognised.

The red and green from holly and the ivy,
amid a blazing fire now roaring lively,
and on the floor were plates of turkey meat,
with brawn and joints of freshly cut lean beef.

Plum puds, mince pies, the biscuits and twelfth cakes,
and chestnuts, apples, cinnamon spiced bakes.
A barrel of fresh oysters, bowls of punch,
Scrooge could not wait to tuck into this lunch."

"I am the ghost of Christmas here and present."
His robe was green, and he seemed very pleasant.
The spirit's eyes were good and kind and clear,
but Scrooge was filled with dreadful fearsome fear.

His face was warm, he smiled behind his eye,
his gentle humour cheerful, spirits high,
the miser touched the ghostly fur-trimmed robe,
and he was whisked outside his own abode.

On Christmas morn, begins our little story . . .
the poulterer sells meat, in splendid glory,
fresh plumbs and spicy coated candied sweets,
and pears, and figs, and sugar almond treats.

The people dressed in waistcoats, look their best,
the merriment was beating in his chest.
Today there is a joy for all to see,
at Christmas there is sherry with our tea.

They came upon a house and knocked the door,
where Cratchit lived in poverty, so poor.
He watched the happy kids sit at the table
and Tiny Tim was clearly not so able.

Bob Cratchit pulled up Tim close to his cheek,
His crippled son was very frail and weak.
"At Christmas God remembers you and me,
to make lame beggars walk and blind men see."

The hot potatoes, goose with little meat,
was served with apple sauce, sage onion treat.
The pudding small, not nearly big enough,
life for the Cratchets, hard and very tough.

"Will Tiny Tim survive? He is so sweet?"
The spirit said, "there is a vacant seat!
A crutch may soon be left without its owner
I didn't think you cared? You are a loaner!"

"As surely he must die, his life must cease!
Decrease the population, be deceased!"
Scrooge hung his head in shame and saddened grief,
he then heard Cratchit raise a glass to speak.

"To Mr Scrooge I will give cheer this year!"
Then Mrs Cratchit frowned at such a cheer
"He is the founder of the feast my dear."
Reluctantly . . . she did not interfere.

The talk of Scrooge had cast disdainful doubt,
but not with cheerful Tiny Tim about.
He toasted Mr Scrooge and they all laughed,
his mood had lifted spirits as time passed!

A tear had welled within the miser's eye.
"Oh surely you do not begin to cry?"
Reminded of his cold and steely nature,
Scrooge felt ashamed and thought of his creator.

The spirit had another scene to share,
his nephew Freddy, who was well aware
of Scrooge's great reluctance to become
a man to celebrate and join the fun.

He heard the laughter, and the merriment,
that rang out from the tiny tenement.
The home was decked in holly red and green,
an atmosphere of fun was what he'd seen.

His niece was very pretty, full of solemn grace,
a small, sweet mouth, and rounded was her face,
with dimpled cheeks and sparkling, sunny eyes,
that melted every heart among he wise.

They spoke of Ebenezer, laughed at him
amusing was his Uncle's soul within,
poor Scrooge was mean and cold and very grim,
but Freddy would defend his Uncle's whim.

As Freddy thought that Scrooge, this very night,
might give his clerk a bonus, make life bright.
A raw of laughter rang with great ferocity,
incapable was Scrooge of generosity.

As Scrooge had softened more into the peace,
the harp so sweetly played by his young niece.
He felt the mourning of the good times lost,
his course seemed doomed and it was at great cost.

The spirit aged now turning grey,
his life was ending soon this very day,
inside his robe there was another shock,
two children, poor and destitute he'd mock.

This little boy is ignorance you see,
this little girl is want, and never will not be free.
they will both die without their dignity
starvation is their crude dark destiny.

"Are there no good workhouses here for free?
resources with a special guarantee?"
The spirit shouted loud and was quite stern
"Just prisons, death and ditches in return."

The Final Ghost

Christmas Future

The clock bell struck at twelve, and made a din,
a hooded phantom then moved straight for him . . .
remembering old Marley's firm prediction,
now Christmas future was his next infliction.

All dressed in black, no eye or face to see,
the silent spirit, still, as he could be . . .
outstretched one hand to point the old man on,
Scrooge trembled as he knew the worst would come.

On hearing happy voices of some men,
"Last night he died, it was about half ten,
I thought he'd never die", they all would laugh.
"No one will mourn for this man's mean evil past."

The room was dark and dank and cold and grim,
a woman sorting out old rags therein,
"Not much to salvage from this mean old miser,"
the dead man lay in bed right there beside her.

The spirit bade old Scrooge to look upon,
though fear had struck him deep, he could not run,
he innocently said, "who cares for him?
A son, or wife, a neighbour, friends within?"

This man to heaven passed without a blessing.
The scene was sad and deeply damned depressing.
The cleaning woman, hard, and showed no feeling.
and no one cared, not one of them was grieving.

But laughter rang out loud inside this house,
No one remembered good from this poor louse,
no tearful eye, or mournful sorry sob,
they were all glad, this man of life was robbed.

The spirit moved along to Cratchit's home,
be-felled in peaceful silence never known.
the children hugged a Father who was crying,
for Tiny Tim had died, no one was smiling.

And Scrooge was very saddened by the news,
his head was in his hands, he'd paid his dues.
If only he had treated Bob more fairly,
he gave him days off, oh so very rarely.

Old Scrooge now saw the error of his ways,
his cruel mean treatment thwarted all his days.
The suffering he had his chance to change,
if some compassion entered his exchange.

"Who was that dead man lying there like stone
without a friend, or loved one to now own?"
To wrought iron gates, the ghost's thin finger pointed,
a church where Scrooge had once been thus anointed.

In dark and spooky, cold and dampened air,
Scrooge couldn't see without a lamp to share,
the ghost now statuesque, and pointed there,
a gravestone now neglected without care.

As Scrooge crept slowly forward, all alone,
he dreaded what he'd see upon the stone,
the name now clear said: "EBENEZER SCROOGE"
and to his knees he buckled with the news.

"Oh no, oh no, I know I can now change!
Of life I am ashamed, I've not engaged!"
The spirit trembled, he would soon be gone,
and Scrooge was left in tears at what he'd done.

Scrooge Redeemed

Poor Scrooge, he held his hands up in a prayer,
the phantom disappeared, no longer there.
he blindly hugged his bedpost in despair,
the fearful ghost had left him crying there.

Excitedly Scrooge sang his plea in key,
"all of these ghostly spirits live in me,
The past, the present and the coming future,
reside in me, forever they will feature."

He ran around like someone who was crazed,
he laughed, he cried, because he was amazed.
"I'm glad" he said, "light as a goose-down feather,
and giddy as a man in rainy weather!"

"A Merry Christmas every year will share,
as each New Year, the world will change out there."
He danced around and skipped and lunged about.
"I've been reborn, of this I have no doubt."

He shouted out, "What day would this day be?"
"It's Christmas Day" a boy replied with glee.
So Scrooge was very glad he hadn't missed-it,
knelt down upon his knees, the floor, he kissed-it!

He called the boy, "Go buy that big old turkey,
that's hanging in the window looking perky,
go get it now, and I'll give you a shilling".
the boy ran off, he was so very willing.

"Deliver it to Crachit's humble place."
He was excited at his brand new pace.
The turkey would be twice the size of Tim!
They'd never know that it was sent from him.

He met the men who asked him for some money,
and Scrooge then laughed, as they believe him merry,
for charity, here is five hundred pounds,
with back-pay, here are silver half a crowns.

His nephew's house, would be his port of call,
"Oh bless my soul, it's Uncle in the hall?"
"Am I invited here for Christmas lunch?
I know I am not due, I'll bring some punch!"

"Of course dear Uncle, please don't ever dither,
I'm glad that you can join us all for dinner."
And Scrooge had such a great time after all,
that he was glad he came and joined the ball.

The morning came, and Scrooge arranged a date,
when Bob arrived, he was a little late.
Scrooge grunted, "And what time do you call this?"
His Clerk apologised, he was remiss.

"I am so sorry Sir, It's once a year!"
"Precisely," Scrooge remarked, "So I'll be clear!
Tomorrow take the day with family,
and I intend to raise your salary. . .

and Merry Christmas too, my fellow Bob."
and over smoking bishop* hearts would throb,
"Make up the fire, and remove your hat,"
together we can have a cosy chat.

And Scrooge was true to his word in the end,
became a decent man, and gained a friend.
A second father to Bob's Tiny Tim,
in turn the fam'ly loved and cared for him.

There was no further intercourse with ghosts,
he kept Christmas alive, and he would boast.
All trace of the cold miser had now gone,
and Tiny Tim said, "God bless everyone."

*(Smoking Bishop is a type of mulled wine)

Author's Biography

Christine was born in Birmingham, in the United Kingdom, where she has spent most of her life. Her passion and love of Poetry started at college when she was lucky enough to have her first poem published, 'The Beach', at the age of seventeen. Since then she has developed her talent for rhyming words, and many more poems have been published with Amazon, Forward Poetry and The United Press.

Her love of stories written by Charles Dickens prompted her to adapt the book "A Christmas Carol" into poetic words, condense it and hopefully make this amazing classical book; fun to read in rhyme.

Christine has written poetry in many different forms, her favourite form is the Sonnet. Her poetry books are all available on Amazon.com.

Christine is also a keen water-colour portrait artist, and has exhibited her paintings abroad. She originally worked as an aerobics fitness instructor for local authority gyms around Birmingham, and also Aston University, before retiring.

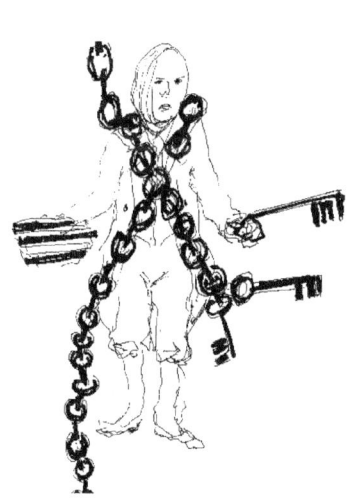

Printed in Great Britain
by Amazon

71019966R00020